A Full Reward

- Meditations from
The Book of Ruth -

Denis A. Wheadon

I0162591

ISBN: 978-1-78364-525-1

www.obt.org.uk

****

The Open Bible Trust
Fordland Mount, Upper Basildon,
Reading, RG8 8LU, UK.

A Full Reward

Meditations from The Book of Ruth

Contents

A Full Reward 4

Introduction

We begin our meditation with a valuable lesson which we learn from the actions of three women who break in upon the scene – Naomi, Orpah and Ruth.

> Naomi said unto her two daughters-in-law, "Go return each to her mother's house: The Lord deal kindly with you" . . . Orpah kissed her mother-in-law: but Ruth clave unto her. (1:8, 14).

The Bible says that as a result of a famine in Judah, and in Bethlehem in particular "a certain man", whose name was Elimelech, took his wife and two sons to Moab, a journey of about fifty miles to the other side of the Dead Sea. One cannot help but wonder whether or not this was a mistake, for things began to go from bad to worse for them in the land of Moab. It would have been better if they had stayed in Bethlehem in spite of the famine. Would God really have seen them starve? I think not!

It would remind us that when we take ourselves out of the will of God we cannot expect things to get better! We are told that Elimelech died in Moab, leaving his widow, Naomi, with her two sons, Mahlon and Chilion. They married two Moabite women, Orpah and Ruth. But tragedy struck again, and they also died, leaving now three widows to face the future alone.

But were they alone? This beautiful story of Ruth demonstrates so perfectly the personal interest and care God has in the affairs of mankind. Naomi may have left her native Judah, but God was also in Moab, and she was never out of His sight, even though she grieved because she felt that the hand of the Lord had gone out against her. How wrong can we sometimes be! As F. B. Meyer so delightfully puts it, this story of Ruth "teaches us that we need never despair of our life, for in ways we know not of, God is bringing good out of evil, and sunshine from the dark and cloudy sky".

Choices

Naomi decided to return to the land of her birth, and in so doing gave her two daughters-in-law a choice as well as providing us with a valuable lesson. She said to the two younger women, "Go, return each to her mother's house: The Lord deal kindly with you . . .": a choice and a blessing! The Bible says that "Orpah kissed her mother-in-law; but Ruth clave unto her". A touching little scene!

Here a choice was given, with the result that one returned to her old way – or perhaps more correctly, she chose to remain in her old way – whilst the other one, Ruth, followed her mother-in-law into a new land, and hence into a completely new way of life.

We are reminded here that the Lord gives us a choice every day either to follow Him or return; in other words, to enter a new life or to remain in our natural, worldly environment. There is no compulsion, except perhaps from our own conviction, but certainly there is none from the

Lord. He gives us a free choice. Ruth was richly blessed because of her decision, as our continued meditation on this Old Testament book will reveal. It was an important decision.

We, too, will be richly blessed if daily we recognise that we have a choice, an important decision to make, that God is giving us that choice, and that we must always be sure to make the right one! Mind you, it is much easier to be like Orpah; it is not so easy to be like Ruth.

The right choice

Ruth, however, made the right choice, the right decision, as subsequent events proved. Although a Moabitess by birth, she was to embrace the Hebrew way of life, and became, in fact, an ancestor of the Lord Jesus Christ Himself (Matthew 1:5). Her plea to her mother-in-law ranks as some of the most beautiful words to be found anywhere in the Bible.

> "Intreat me not to leave thee, or to return from following after thee: for whither thou goest, I will go; and where thou lodgest, I will lodge: thy people shall be my people, and thy God my God." (1:16)

Can we fully appreciate here what it really meant for this young girl to make the decision that she did?

A new land

Ruth was not only about to follow her mother-in-law into a new land, but also into a new way of life. Not only the separation from her own people (for, as far as we know, she had never before been out of Moab), but the loneliness of a foreign land faced her.

A new land, a new way of life, indeed, her decision had far- reaching effects, for everything was going to be new for her. There were to be:

1. new pathways to travel ("for whither thou goest, I will go");
2. a new house and home to live in ("and where thou lodgest, I will lodge");
3. new companions and friends to meet, with whom she would be associated ("thy people shall be my people");
4. and a new source of spiritual power, so very different from the old ("and thy God my God").

Yes, she even acknowledged that she was to have a new God… the One True God – our God, yours and mine! The whole of her life, the whole of her being, the whole of her future was to be completely new.

A new life

Is this not true of us today in a spiritual sense? God is still giving us a choice. The choice is still yours and mine! The truth is, when we made our choice, our decision, to follow the Lord, all things became new – or, at least, they should have done. If the whole of our life, the whole of our being, the whole of our future did not become completely new, something is wrong!

Does our decision to follow the Lord involves us in a new way of living? It should! The old chorus is a perfect illustration of a new way of living.

> Things are different now,
>> something happened to me,
>>> since I gave my heart to Jesus.

> Things are different now,
>> something happened to me,
>>> since I gave my heart to Him

Things I loved before have gone away;
  Things I love far more have come to
  stay
  Things are different now.

Does our decision to follow the Lord result in a new spiritual home? It should! People are social creatures and love to gather together in all sorts of places. The public house, for example, or the social club can become like home to them. For a Christian his church, or chapel, or assembly should become home to him. But more is implied. Not only a new spiritual home where we gather together to worship the Lord, important though this may be, but as the apostle Paul reminds us: "Know ye not that ye are the Temple of God, and that the Spirit of God dwelleth in you?" (1 Corinthians 3:16). We should maintain a new spiritual home where the Spirit of the Lord, Whom we have decided to follow, can dwell at all times.

'Mid all the traffic of the ways,
Turmoils without, within,
Make in my heart a quiet place,
And come and dwell therein:

A little shrine of quietness,
All sacred to Thyself,
Where Thou shalt all my soul possess,
And I may find myself:

A little place of mystic grace,
Of self and sin swept bare,
Where I may look into Thy face,
And talk with Thee in prayer.

Come, occupy my silent place,
And make Thy dwelling there!
More grace is wrought in quietness
Than any is aware.

This prayer of John Oxenham's is particularly appropriate. Our new spiritual home must have an occupant; and our Divine Occupant will enter only if invited!

Does our decision to follow the Lord include new companions and friends? It should! I still remember when I first fully committed my life to the Lord. I was in the Royal Air Force at the time, and my life changed in more ways than one. It only took one to say: "Hey, Wheadon's got religion!" and slowly my Air Force friends began to dwindle away. They even dubbed me the flying parson, making it obvious that I was no longer one of them. Was I lonely? Was I feeling out of it? Not at all! As a result of my commitment I inherited a host of new friends and companions, some of whom are still friends to this day, nearly forty years later!

A new power

Does our decision to follow the Lord acknowledge a new power for living? It should! In those five words uttered by Ruth, her whole life was changed: "and thy God my God". Perhaps she had seen something in Naomi's life which had attracted her to Naomi's God. A lesson here would teach us that, as professing Christians, we have the power to attract people to Christ. We also have the power to repel them! Naomi had obviously created an impression and Ruth had responded. As subsequent events proved, she made the right choice.

In acknowledging Jesus as our Lord and Saviour, we must also acknowledge the power of the Holy Spirit to enable us to live a life acceptable to Him. Without this power we will fail. So when we made our choice, our decision, to follow the Lord, all things became new – above all else, we received this new power for living, which shows how very important it is to make the right choice in the first place. But the story moves on, and with it our meditation.

Kindness and consideration of others never goes unnoticed; and if it is coupled with a strong faith, neither does it go unrewarded, if not by man, always by the Lord; and His rewards are worth far more than man's, anyway!

"The Lord recompense thy work, and a full reward be given thee of the Lord God of Israel, under Whose wings thou art come to trust." (2:12)

Such was the case with Ruth, who, although a stranger in a strange land, found favour not only in the eyes of Boaz, the farmer in whose field she gleaned corn, but also in the eyes of the Lord God of Israel – your God and mine. Her kindness and consideration of Naomi did not go unnoticed or unrewarded, either by Boaz or the Lord.

Here, then, were two widows – both in similar circumstances, one might say, yet in a sense they were totally different. Naomi had returned home and was living in familiar surroundings. Ruth had *adopted* her mother-in-law's homeland, and could therefore be rightly described as "a stranger in a strange land".

A Full Reward

An old law

Being widows, there was little they could do to earn a living, so Ruth took advantage of the law that allowed the poor to glean barley left over from the harvest, and gleaned enough both for herself and for Naomi. In *adopting* a new land she was also able to profit from the law of that land, which stated: ". . . when ye reap the harvest of your land, thou shalt not wholly reap the corners of thy field, neither shalt thou gather the gleanings of thy harvest . . . . thou shalt leave them for the poor and stranger: I am the Lord your God" (Leviticus 19:9-10).

It was not by accident that Ruth began to glean in the field belonging to Boaz, for God still guides those who acknowledge Him, as did this young girl. Boaz was a kinsman (relative) of Elimelech, the late husband of Naomi. He was also a godly man, a caring man, a kind man, which was why Ruth's kindness and consideration of Naomi was noticed by him.

It is impossible to improve on the beautiful language of the Scriptures to illustrate Boaz's attitude and reaction to Ruth. Boaz was a good man, respected by the whole neighbourhood, which in itself recognised Ruth's devotion to her mother-in-law. One might suggest that when Boaz spoke these words to Ruth he was voicing the feelings of the neighbourhood as well as his own.

"It hath been fully shewed me, all that thou hast done unto thy mother-in-law since the death of thine husband: and how thou hast left thy father and thy mother, and the land of thy nativity, and art come unto a people which thou knewest not heretofore. The Lord recompense thy work, and a full reward be given thee of the Lord God of Israel, under whose wings thou art come to trust." (2:11-12).

Such gracious words, acknowledging her decision to embrace a new home, a new people, a new country, but above all a new (to her) God.

Here is yet another valuable lesson for us to learn from this little Book of Ruth; it is a lesson for today. Let us always remember that we are strangers in a strange land. As the old spiritual song puts it: "This world is not my home, I'm just a-passin' through . . ." It is important to realise that the way we live our lives as Christians in this strange land will not go unnoticed or unrewarded, because God's Word says to us today: "A full reward will be given thee of the Lord God."

Even without this added incentive, the world could certainly do with a little more kindness and consideration of others.

Beyond the law

But there is a lesson here also to learn from the actions of Boaz. He went beyond the requirements of the law in showing kindness and consideration for Ruth. His double command to his workers – or rather, the implication of these commands – is worthy of consideration.

". . . reproach her not . . . rebuke her not." (2:15-16)

The law required that he leave only the corners of the field for the poor and stranger to glean (Leviticus 19:9-10). By going beyond the law (not outside the law!) Boaz demonstrated a vital truth that has stood the test of time. Love for God is expressed in kindness and consideration for others, especially those less fortunate than ourselves. Here is a truth which is so often overlooked by Christians today. There is a sense in which we recognise and acknowledge, by our motive and its expression, that "we are labourers together with God" (1 Corinthians 3:9).

The Bible says that, when Ruth went into his field to glean corn, "Boaz commanded his young men, saying, 'Let her glean even among the sheaves and reproach her not'" (2:15). Not just the corners but actually amongst the sheaves! And as if that is not generosity enough, he goes even further when he tells them to "let fall also some of the handfuls on purpose for her, and leave them, that she may glean them, and rebuke her not" (2:16). Not just the corners, not just the sheaves, but a few extras thrown in!

Boaz exemplifies, in his kindness and consideration of Ruth, God's love for mankind. He demonstrates also his own love for God, in that he shows by his actions what privileged people we can be, and how honoured we should feel, to be in the centre of God's will – to be labourers together with God. And, at the risk of repetition, Christians should always recognise that love for God is expressed in kindness and consideration of others. There is always plenty of work for the Christian to do.

Labourers with God

Let us take the Apostle Paul's statement by the way of illustration of this important truth – "we are labourers together with God" (1 Corinthians 3:9). Much of the Welfare State, however much we may criticise it, has its origins in Christian concern for the less fortunate of our country, and so the Parish Poor Fund was set up. Today there are many Christian-based organisations working for the good of our fellowmen, and Christians should be the first to admit that there are many non-Christian organisations also doing good. They serve to complement the Christian's work, not detract from it!

More and more we hear of Christian churches and individuals working together on some projects to alleviate suffering and poverty; groups who come together to bring comfort where needed. Why, then, should the Christian feel privileged and honoured? Paul's statement has the answer. "We are labourers together *with God*". We are demonstrating our love to God by our actions. Not just the corners, not just the sheaves, but a few extras thrown in!

All true Christians should be laborers, never shirking their duty to serve as occasion demands, going the extra mile if necessary; and all true Christians should work together, for we are not rival forces working against each other. If we are, then there is something radically wrong with our Christian experience. The privilege and honour comes in the last two words of Paul's statement – "with God".

We do not work alone, but in company with God, which really means that He is entrusting us with His work. This, of course, includes telling others about Him, by our actions as well as our words, as in the case of Boaz, for instance. True Christians, then, are labourers. They are labourers together.

But above all, they are labourers together *with Almighty God.* And that is certainly a privilege and an honour.

The scene changes, and once again Naomi takes the stage with some timely advice for her daughter-in-law.

> "It is good, my daughter, that thou go out with his maidens, that they meet thee not in any other field." (2:22)

This young girl, Ruth, although a stranger in a strange land, had found favour in the eyes of Boaz, the farmer in whose field she gleaned corn. She had also found favour in the eyes of the Lord, the God in whom she had put her trust. While she continued to glean in the fields of Boaz she reaped a rich reward; while she continued to obey the words of Boaz, when he said to her "Go not to glean in another field", she would continue under his protection.

Obedience

Here was a promise which required a spirit of obedience to activate it; just as the promises of God are sure only to those who believe and obey.

Naomi recognised the implication of the promise and the need to obey, and so advised Ruth accordingly. She said to her "It is good, my daughter, that thou go out with his maidens, that they meet thee not in any other field" (2:22). A complete reading of this short Old Testament book reveals that Ruth obeyed, that she remained faithful, and was richly blessed as a result, for the important phrase was "that they meet thee not in any other field".

Now, what valuable lesson can we learn from this particular phrase? Simply this! Here is a perfect example of what we can expect if we glean in the spiritual fields of the Lord; if we continue to obey His words when He invites us to come to Him and abide with Him. The promise is there, but so must the obedience be! You see, there are many attractive fields where we might glean our pleasures and physical satisfactions, but the rich rewards we glean in the Lord's fields far outweigh any we might find elsewhere.

Out of bounds

But, you may well ask, how do we know which *fields* are acceptable and which ones are *out of bounds?* Some are obvious, others less so. It is the *less so* ones, the so-called *grey* areas, that give the most trouble! This was a question which troubled me when I was a teenager in my church. My parents had forbidden my attending a particular place where I could see no harm in my going. After several arguments we reached stalemate! Then an opportunity presented itself in which I sought to prove my parents' decision wrong!

Once a month, all the ministers of our various churches came together to form a Religious Brains Trust, a Christian version of a popular radio programme of that day. They visited each church in turn, and they were coming to my church that particular month. I would put my question to them. "Is it wrong for me as a Christian to visit . . .?" and I named the place, fully convinced that there was no harm. I was even sure that they would give positive approval. My parents would have a leg to stand on!

The answer, when it finally came, was totally unexpected, and in retrospect, was probably the wisest one I could possibly receive. It went something like this: "We believe that one day the Lord will return – the Second Coming - so the answer is entirely in your hands. We do not know when He will return, only that He will. We also know that He will return suddenly, when you least expect Him, and if you do not mind Him finding you in that place, then by all means go. If you have the slightest doubt, if you would feel even the slightest bit guilty, then it is obviously wrong for you to be there".

What a wise answer! There was no further argument. I never did attend that particular place. In the context of this meditation on Ruth, it would have the wrong *field* for me. I would not have wanted the Lord to find me there! So the message of Ruth is a message for us all. Once again the choice is ours. If, like Ruth, we obey, we remain faithful, we will be richly blessed. May it always be said of us: "It is good . . . that they meet thee not in any other field".

Continuing this theme of obedience, we turn now to Ruth herself. She makes a promise to her mother-in-law, and teaches us a lesson at the same time.

"All that thou sayest unto me I will do." (3:5)

It was said of an Old Testament king that "as long as he sought the Lord, God made him to prosper." (2 Chronicles 26:5). Obedience to God's will and purpose will always result in blessings, either in this life or the next. Such was the case of Ruth, in our continuing story of this young girl, who promised Naomi that she would obey her every word. "All that thou sayest unto me I will do", she said, and she meant it, for she went to Boaz, the farmer who had been so kind to her, and lay down at his feet – nowhere else! This was important.

A point of law

Under Hebrew law the next kinsman in line had to be given the right to purchase the land and possessions of the one who had died, and that included the widow, if there was one. Ruth was a young widow, but by her strict obedience she did not encourage Boaz to be dishonourable, so that he was unable to acknowledge the right of a kinsman actually nearer than himself. If Ruth had not obeyed Naomi's instructions to the letter, Boaz might have weakened and failed to fulfil the law. There would have been no blessing to follow, only guilt.

No doubt there are many excellent expositions available on the Book of Ruth should the reader wish to study the law or history of this period. However, that is not the purpose of this booklet, which is a meditation seeking to make the Bible relevant to our present situation. The lesson to learn from this incident is not the intricacy of Hebrew law, important though that may be, but something much more fundamental. Indeed, the lesson for us is plain enough.

Application

If we would be blessed in our daily living, then in obedience to the Lord's word to us (what He says in the Bible for us today; what He is saying to us all through this meditation on the book of Ruth) we must always be ready to say: "All that thou sayest unto me I will do"; and the important word, of course, is *all!*

The apostle Paul, writing to the Christians who lived in Rome, encouraged them to "rejoice with them that do rejoice, and weep with them that weep" (Romans 12:15). This is exactly what the women of Israel did when Ruth and Boaz became the proud parents of a baby son. There was great rejoicing.

> Blessed be the Lord, Which hath not left thee this day without a kinsman, that His name may be famous in Israel. (4:14)

There are two ways of doing just about everything – the right way and the wrong way! Throughout the devotional meditation on the Book of Ruth three main characters have featured: they are Naomi, Ruth, and Boaz. And in that order, beginning with Naomi, they did things the right way. They made the right choices. They obeyed the laws of God. And untold blessing followed.

Indeed, there were others who witnessed this, who rejoiced with Naomi as she rejoiced, for, as the Bible says, "the women said unto Naomi, Blessed be the Lord, Which hath not left thee this day without a kinsman, that his name may be famous in Israel" (4:14). If any of the three had failed there would have been no blessing for the others. Each depended on the other, often without realising it.

Also, without knowing it, Ruth was to find a place in the genealogy of the Davidic line by which the Lord Jesus Christ came! Had she not obeyed, this important link would have been broken.

The lesson for us to learn from this is an important one; it is that, not only must we be obedient to the Lord's will for us personally in all things, doing those things in the right way, at the right time, in the right place, and thereby being blessed, but we are responsible for each other, perhaps sometimes without realising it!

This really sums up all the lessons we have learned from the Book of Ruth in this devotional meditation. Our disobedience would result in blessing being denied to someone else. It works the other way as well! Ruth's blessing of a son, which is what caused the women of Israel to rejoice with the words they expressed to Naomi, was in fact Naomi's blessing as well as a blessing to Boaz.

Who knows just how our blessings may bless others!

Summary

Naomi said unto her two daughters-in-law, "Go, return each to her mother's house: the Lord deal kindly with you" ... Orpah kissed her mother-in-law, but Ruth clave unto her. (1:8-14)

Here a choice was given, which reminds us that the Lord gives us a choice every day, either to follow Him or reject Him. Ruth was richly blessed when she made the right choice; so will we be if we recognise that we also have a choice and make the right one by following the Lord.

"Intreat me not to leave thee, or to return from following after thee: for wither thou goest, I will go; and where thou lodgest, I will lodge: thy people shall be my people, and thy God my God." (1:16)

Having made the right choice, as with Ruth, we are involved in a totally new way of living – a new spiritual home, new companions and friends, but above all, a new source of spiritual power to live that new life. This is why it is so important to make the right choice in the first place.

> "The Lord recompense thy work, and a full reward be given thee of the Lord God of Israel, under whose wings thou art come to trust." (2:12)

Kindness and consideration of others never goes unnoticed; coupled with a strong faith, neither does it go unrewarded by the Lord. Ruth's new way of living led her into a new land, a strange land. Christians, too, are passing through this world, a strange land indeed! Our kindness and consideration of others will not go unnoticed, and like Ruth, "a full reward will be given thee of the Lord God". Even without this added incentive, this world could certainly do with a little more kindness and consideration of others.

> "Reproach her not . . . rebuke her not." (2:15-16)

A Full Reward   44

Boaz demonstrates by his double command a vital truth, which should be the hallmark of every true Christian today who has recognised that he has a choice. Such a Christian will have made the right choice and is now following the Lord, and is involved in a totally new way of living. That way of living acknowledges that love for God is expressed in kindness and consideration for others, especially those less fortunate than themselves In all this "we are labourers together with God" and that, indeed, is both a privilege and an honour.

> "It is good, my daughter, that thou go out with his maidens, that they meet thee not in any other field." (2:22)

When we take the right decision, it involves us in a totally new way of living; all the blessings of that new way of life are ours; all the promises of God are sure to those who believe and obey. Yes God's promises require a spirit of obedience to activate them. Our new fields of service will only become fields of blessing if we remain in them. To seek for blessings in other fields will result only in misery. Our decision to follow the Lord in the new land requires obedience to His will with no turning back to the old land where we would not like the Lord to find us when He comes again!

"All that thou sayest unto me I will do." (3:5)

If we would be blessed in our daily living as we travel this new land, as we glean our pleasures in the new fields and as we seek to show God's love by our kindness and consideration of others, then in obedience to the Lord's word to us, what He says to us from the Bible and what He may be saying to us through this devotional meditation in the Book of Ruth, we will always be ready to say, Lord, "All that thou sayest . . ."

> "Blessed by the Lord, which hath not left thee this day without a kinsman, that his name may be famous in Israel." (4:14)

Ruth began by making the right decision. She involved herself in a totally new way of living, which finally led to a time a great rejoicing, and sums up all the lessons we have learned from our devotional meditation of the Book of Ruth. Not only must we make the right decision in the first place, not only must we be obedient to the Lord's will for us personally in all things, doing those things in the right way, at the right time, in the right place, and thereby being blessed, but we are also responsible for each other. Our disobedience could result in denied blessing to someone else. Our obedience . . . well, who knows just how our blessings may bless others with a full reward.

More on Ruth

Studies in Ruth

Michael Penny

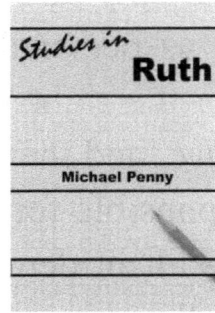

**Esther and Ruth
by Charles Ozanne**

There are two books in the Bible which take their names from women, Esther and Ruth. The first was a Jew, the second a Gentile.

The author sees these two women as types of the Israel of God. He paints many parallels and draws many similarities between events in their personal lives and the experiences of the Jewish and Gentile Christians of the Acts period.

These booksare also available as eBooks from Amazon and Apple, and as KDP paperbacks from Amazon.

Studies in Ruth
By Michael Penny

"The story of Ruth is one of the most loved in the Old Testament. Its peaceful pastoral atmosphere, the nobility and faithfulness of its leading characters, a happy outcome from a background of exile and affliction, these are some of the features which have endeared this short narrative to Christian readers of all times. When the surface meaning is so delightful there may seem no occasion to look for a deeper meaning in the story."

So wrote Charles Ozanne in his book *Esther and Ruth*.

Without in the slightest disagreeing with the above, the author, in these *Studies in Ruth*, goes somewhat deeper and in so doing enables the reader to find greater depth of character in both Ruth and Boaz. And in doing so, the reader will gain a greater appreciation of their situation and predicament.

About the author

Denis Wheadon was born in Dorset in 1931. He was educated at Foster's Grammar School in Sherborne and later trained as a commercial artist and industrial illustrator. He did his national service in the RAF, and on leaving worked in the education department of the UK Atomic Energy Authority, before going to theological college and being ordained in 1954. He was a regular broadcaster on Two Counties Radio with Pause Awhile from 1983-1991, and owned a Christian Hotel with a daily Christian ministry.

Other works by Denis Wheadon include:

The Land of Spiritual Experience – Deuteronomy
In the Beginning – Genesis 1
In My Father's House – John 13-17
Cameos in Colossians
A Full Reward – Ruth

Details of these can be seen on
www.obt.org.uk

Cameos in Colossians

Meditations from Paul's Letter to the Colossians

Colossians

Denis Wheadon

In the Beginning

A Study of Genesis 1:1-5

Denis A Wheadon

The Land of Spiritual Experience

Meditations in Deuteronomy

Denis Wheadon

In My Father's House

Meditations from John chapters 13-17

Denis Wheadon

A Full Reward

Meditations from The Book of Ruth

Denis Wheadon

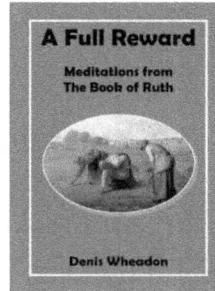

Details of the books mentioned on these pages
can be seen on **www.obt.org.uk**
They can be ordered from that website and also
from

The Open Bible Trust,
Fordland Mount, Upper Basildon,
Reading, RG8 8LU, UK.

They are also available as eBooks from Amazon
and Apple,
and as KDP paperbacks from Amazon

**For a full list of books available
from
The Open Bible Trust,
please visit**

www.obt.org.uk

Search magazine

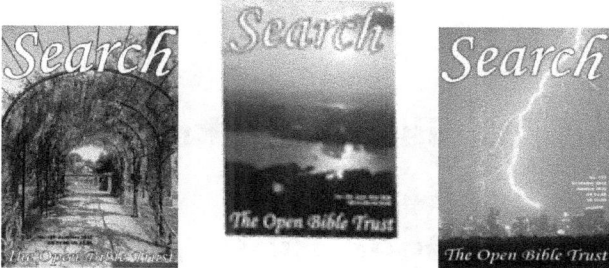

For a free sample of
the Open Bible Trust's magazine *Search,*
email

admin@obt,org.uk

or visit

www.obt.org.uk/search

**For a full list of books available from
The Open Bible Trust,
please visit**

www.obt.org.uk

About this book

A Full Reward
Meditations from the Book of Ruth

In his last letter the apostle Paul tells us not only that "All Scripture is God-breathed", but also that all Scripture "is useful for teaching, rebuking, correcting and training in righteousness". All this is so that "the man of God may be thoroughly equipped for every good work" (2 Timothy 3:16-17).

Thus there is a message for everyone of us in every book of the Bible, and occasionally such messages can come from the most unexpected places. One such place is the Old Testament book of Ruth. It is one of those books which you can take and read through in less than fifteen minutes at one sitting. Situated between the longer books of Judges and 1 Samuel, it has but four short chapters, although its brevity in no way diminishes its significance or its value.

To obtain the maximum benefit from this devotional study it is suggested that the book of Ruth be read first.

For a full list of books available from The Open Bible Trust, please visit

www.obt.org.uk

Publications of The Open Bible Trust must be in accordance with its evangelical, fundamental and dispensational basis. However, beyond this minimum, writers are free to express whatever beliefs they may have as their own understanding, provided that the aim in so doing is to further the object of The Open Bible Trust. A copy of the doctrinal basis is available at

www.obt.org.uk/doctrinal-basis

or from:

THE OPEN BIBLE TRUST
Fordland Mount, Upper Basildon,
Reading, RG8 8LU, GB

www.ingramcontent.com/pod-product-compliance
Lightning Source LLC
Chambersburg PA
CBHW060611030426
42337CB00018B/3048